EXPLORE
NIGHT
SCIENCE!

CINDY BLOBAUM

Illustrated by Bryan Stone

For Anna, who is always ready to stay up late and explore the night.

Nomad Press
A division of Nomad Communications
10 9 8 7 6 5 4 3 2 1

Manufactured by Thomson-Shore, Dexter, MI (USA)
October 2012, RMA584HS418
ISBN: 978-1-61930-156-6

Illustrations by Bryan Stone
Educational Consultant, Marla Conn

Questions regarding the ordering of this book should be addressed to
Independent Publishers Group
814 N. Franklin St.
Chicago, IL 60610
www.ipgbook.com

Nomad Press
2456 Christian St.
White River Junction, VT 05001
www.nomadpress.net

CONTENTS

Titles in the **Explore Your World!** Series

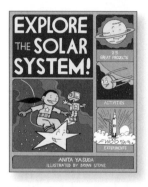   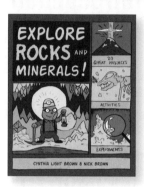

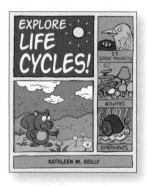   

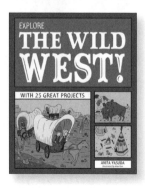 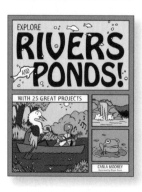  

Introduction

Open the door after the sun goes down and before it rises again. Step out into the dark. Most colors look gray or black. Do sounds jump out at you? Do smells seem stronger? How does the air feel? Is it different from the way it feels during the day?

WORDS TO KNOW

night: the time after the sun sets and before the sun rises, when it is dark.

migrate: to move from one place to another.

Night is different from day, whether you live in the country or in a city. What you see in the sky changes. Different animals are active. Different plants bloom. And what happens at night changes with every season of the year. Star gazing and owl calling are best on winter nights. Moth catching and bat watching are summer night activities. Spring and fall are when many animals have babies or **migrate**, often when it is dark.

What do you need to explore **night science**? Mostly, you need your **senses**. Your eyes, ears, nose, and skin are your most important tools. The way you see, hear, smell, and feel changes at night. By testing your senses in the dark, you'll learn how to improve them and use them better.

When should you explore the night? Some night scientists stay up late. They do their studies after it gets dark. Other night scientists wake up early. They do their studies before it gets light.

You'll discover that some nights are longer than others. During winter, long nights mean you don't have to stay up too late or wake up too early to do your experiments. But not everything happens on winter nights. Plan some exploring time for weekends in the other seasons. Then you can sleep during the day if you're tired from staying up late.

Just for FUN!

HOW DO YOU GO FOR DAYS WITHOUT SLEEP AND NEVER FEEL TIRED?

Sleep at night!

Most of the activities in this book work best in the dark. But before you start, get the materials ready where it is light.

While some activities should be done outside, others can be done inside in a dark room or basement. It's usually okay if there is a little light. Most nights aren't completely dark either.

Night is your chance to explore a new world. You don't have to travel far. You don't need tools that cost a lot of money. And you might even discover a whole new world!

WORDS TO KNOW

supernova: an exploding star.

galaxy: a group of millions or billions of stars. The earth is in a galaxy called the Milky Way.

light year: a unit of measure for very long distances. One light year is the distance that light travels in a year, about 6 trillion miles (9.5 trillion kilometers).

SUPERNOVA DISCOVERY

Kids can be night scientists! In January 2011, a 10-year-old girl named Kathryn Aurora Gray from New Brunswick, Canada, became the youngest person to discover a **supernova**. Scientists find supernovas by comparing photos taken on different nights in far-away **galaxies**.

Kathryn and her dad were looking at 52 photos taken of the night sky in a galaxy 240 million **light years** away. Kathryn noticed a new light in the fourth picture and asked her father, "Is that one?" After more research, she and her dad were sure. Kathryn became the first person to identify the supernova known as SN2010lt that exploded 240 million years ago.

When and Why Is It Night?

Night starts when the sun disappears below the **horizon**. Some light stays in the sky for a while. This time is called **dusk**. Night ends when the sun peeks above the horizon. There may already be some light in the sky even before the sun moves above the horizon. This time is called **dawn**. The light you see at dusk and dawn is called **twilight**.

WORDS TO KNOW

horizon: the line that separates the land from the sky.

dusk: the time after the sun goes below the horizon, when there is still sunlight in the sky.

dawn: the time before the sun rises above the horizon, when there is sunlight in the sky.

twilight: light that is visible in the sky at dawn and dusk, when the sun is below the horizon.

WORDS TO KNOW

atmosphere: the layer of gases that wraps around the earth.

water vapor: water as a gas, like fog, steam, or mist.

There is twilight because Earth has an **atmosphere**. Our atmosphere is like an invisible blanket wrapped around the planet. The sun's rays bounce off the air, water, clouds, and dust that make up the blanket of the atmosphere. Some of that bouncing light comes down to Earth where you can see it in the sky.

The more things that are in the atmosphere near you, the more it splits the sunlight into different colors. So if there is a lot of smoke from a fire or **water vapor** in the atmosphere, the clouds and sky at twilight might have shades of purple, pink, red, and orange.

Just for FUN!

WHAT DID THE ATMOSPHERE SAY TO EARTH?

"I've got you covered!"

DID YOU KNOW?

Some people use the color of the sky at dusk and dawn to predict the weather. Here's an old sailor's saying:

Red sky in the morning, sailors take warning. (A storm is coming.)

Red sky at night, sailors delight. (The weather will be good.)

Observe the twilight sky colors and then see if it is true!

Animals and plants use the amount of light as a **cue** to what they should do. Why are dusk and dawn some of the most active times in nature? Living things that have been active for hours get ready to rest. Living things that have been resting start getting active. Some flowers are opening while others are closing. Insects buzz, click, and chirp. Bats and night hawks swoop around to find a meal. Birds sing. Stars appear or disappear.

There is a lot going on at dusk and dawn, and usually just enough light to see things clearly. Twilight is a great time to start exploring the night.

HOW LONG IS NIGHT?

Nights can be long, short, or always the same. It depends on where you live and the time of year. You can't feel it, but Earth is like a big ball that is always spinning. Every 24 hours the earth spins around one time. This equals one calendar day.

As the earth spins, it is also moving in a circle around the sun. This circle is called Earth's **orbit**. As Earth moves through its orbit, different parts of it tilt toward the sun.

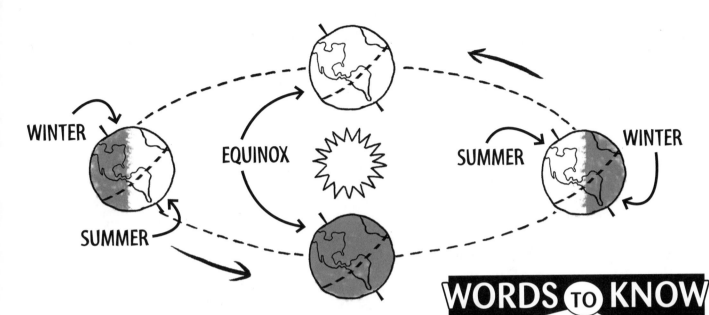

WINTER

EQUINOX

SUMMER

WINTER

SUMMER

When the part of Earth where you live is tilted toward the sun, you get longer days and shorter nights. This happens in summer. When your part of Earth is tilted away from the sun, you get shorter days and longer nights. This happens in winter. If you live near the **equator**, in a place like Quito, Ecuador, you always have days and nights that are 12 hours long.

Every year around March 21 and September 23, the length of day and night are the same, all around the world. This is because on those dates, the earth is not tilting toward or away from the sun. These are called the spring and fall **equinoxes**. They mark the official beginning of the seasons autumn and spring. On an equinox, the sun appears to rise directly in the east, and set directly in the west.

WORDS TO KNOW

equator: an imaginary line around the middle of the earth that divides it in two halves.

equinox: a Latin word than means "equal night." The spring equinox is around March 21 and the fall equinox is around September 23. On these two days each year, day and night are 12 hours long all around the world.

7

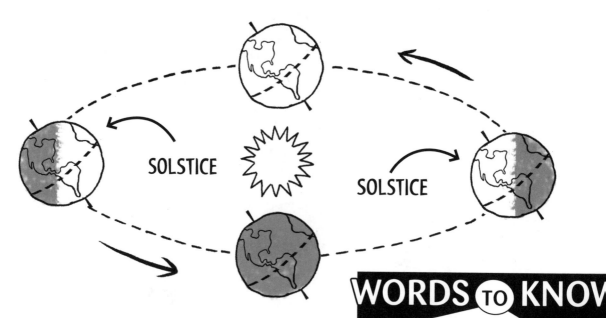

SOLSTICE

SOLSTICE

December 21 and June 21 are two other important dates. These dates are called the **solstices**.

The summer solstice marks the longest day and shortest night of the year and the start of summer. This happens when the part of Earth you live on is tilted as far toward the sun as it will go. The sun will seem to rise from the northeast and set in the northwest.

The winter solstice marks the shortest day and longest night of the year. It is the start of winter. This happens when the part of Earth you live on is tilted as far away from the sun as it will go. The sun will seem to rise from the southeast and set in the southwest.

ACTIVITY: **Light and the Atmosphere**

See how light bounces off the atmosphere. Do this at night or in a place that can be made very dark.

1 Put the black paper at the edge of a table. The edge of the table is like the horizon. Put the tub on the paper.

2 Fill the tub about three-quarters full with water and sprinkle nutmeg on top. The tub, water, and nutmeg make the atmosphere.

3 Turn on the flashlight. Hold the flashlight below the horizon. Aim the light up toward the tub. Slowly move the flashlight up toward the horizon. Watch what happens in, under, and behind the tub.

4 Try the test again with just the paper on the table. What do you notice when the atmosphere is gone?

DID YOU KNOW?

The moon does not have an atmosphere. This means there is no twilight on the moon. When the sun sets below the moon's horizon, it is instantly dark. When the sun rises above the horizon, it is instantly light.

ACTIVITY: **Night Watch**

SUPPLIES

- ⬧ 2 thin, 9-inch paper plates (23 centimeters)
- ⬧ scissors
- ⬧ black pen
- ⬧ ruler
- ⬧ pencil
- ⬧ pin
- ⬧ paper fastener
- ⬧ blue and yellow highlighters

When does your night start? It can change every season. One way to keep track is to make your own night watch.

1 Fold both plates in half. Fold them in half again. Each plate should look like a big piece of pie.

2 Open up each plate. There are four equal sections. Cut one section out of one plate, leaving the inside corner uncut. This is your window plate. Set it aside.

3 Using the black pen, trace the section lines on the uncut plate. At the outer edge, label each section with the name of one season: Winter, Spring, Summer, Fall. This is your record plate. You will record what you learn about night science on this plate.

4 Put the ruler along one dark line. Starting at the center, make a little pencil dot every ¼ inch all the way across (every ½ centimeter). Repeat along the other dark lines. Connect the dots to make circles around the plate.

5 Use the pin to poke a hole through the center of each plate. Put the window plate on top. Push the paper fastener through the holes to connect the plates.

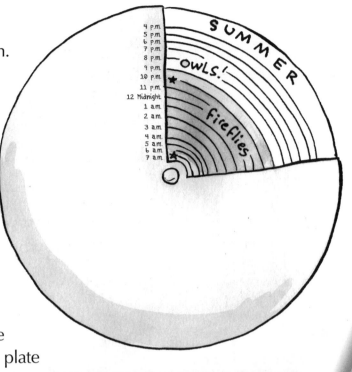

6 On the window plate, write 7 a.m. by the line closest to the center of the record plate. Write 6 a.m. by the next line out, then 5 a.m., 4 a.m., 3 a.m., 2 a.m., 1 a.m., 12 midnight, 11 p.m., 10 p.m., 9 p.m., 8 p.m., 7 p.m., 6 p.m., 5 p.m., 4 p.m. You can add more time circles if you live near the North or South Pole.

7 Dial the window plate so the current season is showing. Look at a clock when the sun is setting. Make a small star on the line on the record plate that matches that time. In the morning, look at a clock when the sun is rising. Make a small star on the line on the record plate that matches that time. Color the lines between the two stars with the blue highlighter. Color the lines above and below the stars with the yellow highlighter. Do this at least once every season.

WORDS TO KNOW

meteor: the streak of light when a small rock or piece of dust burns up as it enters the earth's atmosphere. We see it as a shooting star.

8 Use your night watch to help you remember when to listen for owls, look for fireflies, watch a **meteor** shower, or smell night plants blooming. Add notes between the lines or on the back recording the things you do and learn about night.

CLASSROOM CONNECTION: Share your night watch with your classmates. Find out if your friends are noticing the same or different things as you are at night.

ACTIVITY: **Night Length**

Hold the earth in your hands as you spin a ball and walk around the sun to see how the length of night is different in different seasons and on different parts of the earth. Think about where on the globe it is night when you are in daytime. Think about where on the globe it is winter when you are in summer.

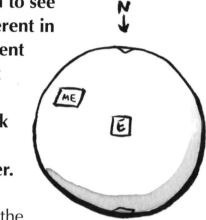

WORDS (TO) KNOW

North Pole: the most northern point on the earth.

South Pole: the most southern point on the earth.

1 Use the pen to label the stickers **North Pole** (N), **South Pole** (S), Equator (E), and "Me".

2 The ball is Earth. Use the N and S stickers to mark the North and South Poles on opposite sides of the ball. Put the E sticker halfway between the North and South poles. This sticker marks the equator. Look at a world map and find where you live in relation to the poles and the equator. Put the Me sticker to mark where you live.

3 If your lamp has a shade, take it off. Turn on the lamp. This is your sun. Turn off all the other lights around you.

4 Hold the ball on the N and S stickers. Start with the Me sticker facing the sun. Turn the ball one time all the way around as you count to 24. This is the 24 hours in one calendar day.

DID YOU KNOW?

Winter at the North Pole and South Pole is very dark. Each year there are 179 days when the sun never rises above the horizon. That means it is night half the year!

5 Turn the ball again at the same speed. This time, count how many seconds the "Me" sticker is in the dark. That is how many hours it is night.

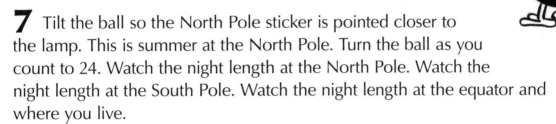

6 Now walk around the lamp as you spin the ball. Your walking path is Earth's orbit around the sun.

7 Tilt the ball so the North Pole sticker is pointed closer to the lamp. This is summer at the North Pole. Turn the ball as you count to 24. Watch the night length at the North Pole. Watch the night length at the South Pole. Watch the night length at the equator and where you live.

8 Tilt the ball so the South Pole sticker is tilted towards the lamp. Turn the ball as you count to 24. Watch the night length at the South Pole and at the other stickers. Now you can see why day and night last half the year at the North and South Poles. Does it make sense now that day and night at the equator is always the same?

CALENDAR + BOOK = ALMANAC

An almanac is both a calendar and a book. Almanacs have charts of when the sun, moon, stars, and planets rise and set for every day of the year. Printed almanacs have been around since 1457. Long before there were almanacs, people watched when and where the sun, moon, stars, and planets rose and set. They made big circles of stones on the ground. The stones lined up with the rising and setting places in the sky. There are circles of stones like this all around the world. The most famous one is Stonehenge in England.

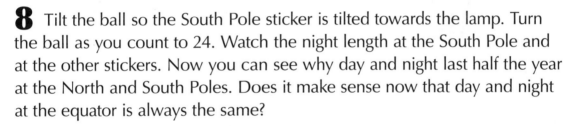

Seeing the Night

During the day, you rely on your sense of sight. When there is light, your eyes see colors, shapes, motion, and distance.

When you first step into the dark, can you see colors, shapes, motion, and distance in the same way? Probably not. You might even find yourself off balance! Many people feel off balance when they can't see things around them. Have you ever noticed that it's harder to walk in the dark?

HOW EYES WORK

Why don't your eyes see well at night? It helps to know how your eyes work. Look at your eyes in a mirror. In the middle you will see a black hole. This hole is called the **pupil**. Around the pupil is a ring of color. That ring is called the **iris**. The iris contains a muscle. When it's dark, the iris muscle pulls on the pupil to make it bigger. This lets more light into your eye. When it's very bright, the iris pushes in on the pupil to make it smaller. This lets less light into your eye.

The light that comes in the pupil goes to the **retina**. The retina is like a screen at the back of the eye. It has two main kinds of **cells** called **cone cells** and **rod cells**. These cells are **sensitive** to light.

WORDS TO KNOW

pupil: the opening that lets light into the eye.

iris: a part of the eye with a muscle that is seen as a ring of color.

retina: the light-sensitive lining at the back of the eye.

cell: the most basic part of a living thing. Billions of cells make up a plant or animal.

cone cell: a cone-shaped cell in the retina that is sensitive to bright light and color.

rod cell: a rod-shaped cell in the retina that is sensitive to low light. It cannot pick up colors.

sensitive: easily affected by something.

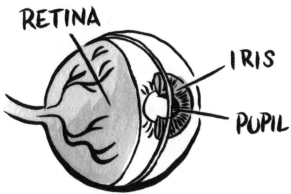

BIG PUPIL, LITTLE PUPIL

TRY THIS

In a room with light, hold a hand over one eye for 10 minutes. Look in a mirror. Take your hand away from your eye. Look at the size of the pupil in each eye. How are they different?

Now cover your eye again for another 10 minutes. When the time is up, go into a dark room. Look around with your uncovered eye. Cover that eye as you uncover the other one. Notice how much more you can see with the eye that has a big pupil. For more fun, blink back and forth between each eye.

TRY THIS

WORDS TO KNOW

mammal: an animal that has a constant body temperature and is mostly covered with hair or fur. Humans, dogs, horses, and mice are mammals.

reptile: an animal covered with scales that crawls on its belly or on short legs. A reptile changes its body temperature by moving to warmer or cooler places. Snakes, turtles, lizards, alligators, and crocodiles are reptiles.

amphibian: an animal with moist skin that is born in water but lives on land. An amphibian changes its body temperature by moving to warmer or cooler places. Frogs, toads, newts, efts, and salamanders are amphibians.

Cone cells are found in the middle of the retina. They detect colors and details. Cone cells need bright light to work. When it's light, you see things best that are right in front of you. The more types of cone cells you have, the more types of colors you can see. Many **mammals** have only two types of cone cells. Humans and most monkeys have three. Most birds, **reptiles** and **amphibians** have four cone types. Some butterflies have five and the mantis shrimp may have up to 12.

Rod cells are found around the cone cells. They send cues about the shape of things and motion to the brain. Rod cells can work in very dim light. You've probably noticed that after you are in the dark for a little while, you start to see better. This is because it takes about 20 minutes of being in the dark before rod cells work their best.

WORDS TO KNOW

peripheral: at the side or edge of something.

nocturnal: active at night.

adaptation: something that helps a plant or animal survive.

DID YOU KNOW?

Why did pirates wear an eye patch? So one eye would always be ready to see in low light. Since pirates often moved from the bright deck of the ship to down below where it was dark, they needed to be able to see well in both bright and dark light. Instead of waiting for their eyes to adjust when they went below, they would simply lift their eye patch.

Have you ever noticed that when it's dark, it's easiest to see things out of the sides of your eyes? It's because that is where your rod cells are. This is called your **peripheral** vision. The eyes of most **nocturnal** animals have **adaptations** to see at night. Many of these animals don't have any cone cells in their eyes so they can't see any colors. Everything looks white, gray, or black. But nocturnal animals have lots of rod cells in their eyes.

TRY THIS

BALANCE CHALLENGE

In a room with light, count how many seconds you can stand on one leg with your eyes open. Is it the same for each leg? Go to a very dark place and try again.

TRY THIS

OTHER ADAPTATIONS

WORDS TO KNOW

reflect: to redirect something that hits a surface, such as heat, light, or sound.

Most nocturnal animals have large eyes with a wide pupil. An owl's eyes are so big they fill half of its head. Have you ever noticed the glowing eyes of a cat or deer caught in the lights of your car? Nocturnal animals have a thick layer beneath their retina that **reflects** light like a mirror. It helps them use what little light they have to see better. And it makes their eyes appear to glow when bright light shines on them in the dark.

Some nocturnal animals even have their eyes on the sides of their heads. This adaptation gives these animals better peripheral vision so they can see if anything is sneaking up on them.

DID YOU KNOW?

Have you ever heard the saying "blind as a bat?" It's not true! The eyes of bats have lots more rod cells than cone cells, which makes sense. But even if they are flying around during the day, their eyes work just fine.

But since only one eye sees things on each side, these animals have trouble with **depth perception**. Poor depth perception makes it hard to know how close something is and how fast it is moving.

Have you ever noticed that a cat's pupils are shaped like a vertical line? That's because cats need to move around during the day and at night. A slit-shaped pupil protects a cat's eyes in daylight from too much light. But it also means that the pupil can become very large in dim light. This gives cats excellent night vision.

In the daytime, a small round pupil would cover up rod cells on the retina, making cats less sensitive to moving things. But a slit-shaped pupil lets light in to at least some of the rod cells. Kangaroos, sheep, goats, foxes, and some snakes also have slit-shaped pupils.

At night it's hard to see colors or details. It's easy to get frightened of dark shapes that are moving. Some dark shapes you see are **shadows**. Other dark shapes you see are **silhouettes**. You will be a better night scientist when you learn the shadows and silhouettes of common nocturnal animals.

WORDS TO KNOW

depth perception: being able to tell how close or far away something is.

shadow: an area that looks dark because something is between it and the light.

silhouette: a real object that looks dark because the light is behind it.

IMPROVE YOUR NIGHT VISION

For a long time, people have wanted to see better at night. Maybe your mom or dad has said, "Eat more carrots if you want to see at night." Carrots contain something called carotene. It's what makes a carrot orange. Your body turns carotene into vitamin A. Vitamin A is used by your retina to send signals to your brain. So carrots are good for your eyes, but you probably get enough vitamin A even without eating an extra helping of carrots.

Just for FUN!

WHAT IS AS BIG AS AN ELEPHANT BUT DOESN'T WEIGH ANYTHING?

Its shadow!

What can you do to help your night vision? You could use a night vision scope, binoculars, or a low-light camera. Scientists have developed several different devices to help them see better at night.

IMAGE INTENSIFIERS like night goggles increase the amount of energy made by the light coming in, like starlight or moonlight. When you look through the device, the images on the screen glow brighter than what you see with your eyes alone.

WORDS TO KNOW

light source: the place where light is coming from.

THERMAL IMAGING DETECTORS can make images even when there is no natural light at all. Instead of using light, they sense the heat given off by objects and make an electronic image out of it. Sometimes these images show cold objects as black and hot objects as white. But some thermal cameras create colorful images of blues, yellows, reds, oranges, blacks, and whites.

NEAR-INFRARED ILLUMINATORS, like the Sony NightShot camcorder, send out light signals that are invisible to most humans and animals. The near-infrared light bounces off objects and comes back to the lens. This makes a much better image in low-light video scenes than would be possible without the extra **light source**.

DID YOU KNOW?

There are some moths and dung beetles that have full-color vision at night. Scientists are studying how their eyes work. They want to use that information to invent better night vision cameras.

These inventions are used on army tanks, airplanes, and security cameras. Search-and-rescue teams, wildlife biologists, Special Forces teams, and sleep scientists also use them. People may look funny when they are wearing one, but think of all the things they can see!

ACTIVITY: **Color Challenge**

Can you see colors at night? Try this to find out.

1 Start in a place with good lighting. Peel the paper wrappers off the crayons.

2 Number the pieces of white paper 1, 2, 3, and 4. Put them on the clipboard with page 1 on top.

3 On page 1, use each crayon to write its color. Use the red crayon to write R-E-D, etc. Turn the paper over and put it on the bottom of the stack.

4 Now go to a dark room. On page 2, use each crayon to write its color. After you have used all nine crayons, turn over the piece of paper. Put it on the bottom.

5 On page 3, use ALL the crayons to draw a picture. Take your time! Turn over page 3. Put it on the bottom. And on page 4, use each crayon to write its color again.

6 Now go back to the well-lit area. Place pages 1, 2, and 4 side by side. Look at which colors you got right and which ones you got wrong. Did your color vision get better from page 2 to page 4? The time you took to draw your picture on page 3 gave your eyes time to adjust to the low light.

DID YOU KNOW?

For many years, most fire trucks were red. The color red is often used to warn people of danger and is easy to see during the day. But red turns black in low light, making red fire trucks hard to see at night. Lime green and yellow are the colors most visible to the human eye. Now many fire trucks are bright yellow or have yellow patches on them to make them easier to see at night.

ACTIVITY: **Open, Shut Them**

Try catching a ball with your eyes open and then with one eye closed in different lighting. You'll see what it feels like to be an animal with eyes on the side of its head.

SUPPLIES

✧ paper
✧ pencil
✧ light-colored ball

1 On your paper, make a chart like the one below to record your results.

2 When it's daylight, grab your ball and your chart and head outside. Throw the ball high up in the air. Catch it when it comes down. Count how many throws it takes before you catch the ball 10 times. Record that number on your chart.

3 Now close one eye. Throw the ball high in the air. Catch it when it comes down. Record the total number of throws you make before you catch the ball 10 times.

4 Do the same two tests in the dark, first with both eyes open, then with one eye open.

5 Look at your results. Did you make more throws in the light or in the dark? With one eye open or both eyes open? What does this teach you about depth perception?

LIGHTING AND EYES	NUMBER OF THROWS BEFORE 10 CATCHES
In the light – both eyes open	
In the light – one eye open	
In the dark – both eyes open	
In the dark – one eye open	

ACTIVITY: **Silhouettes and Shadows**

Learn how to make animal silhouettes and shadows using stuffed animals and with your own two hands!

1 Put the flashlight on a table about 4 feet away from a wall (just over 1 meter). The light should point toward the wall. You can move the light closer or farther away if you need to.

2 Turn on the flashlight to see where the light shines. Tape a piece of paper to the wall so the light shines on it.

3 Put one stuffed animal between the light and the wall. Move near the wall and look back at the animal toward the light. The dark shape you see is its silhouette. Now move behind the animal and look at the wall. The dark image on the wall is its shadow. Move the animal closer to the wall. Does the shadow get bigger or smaller?

4 Place the animal and light so the whole shadow is on the paper. Use the crayon to trace around the shadow. Color in the shadow so it is all one color. Write the name of the animal on the back of the paper.

SILHOUETTE

SHADOW

5 Put a new piece of paper on the wall for each stuffed animal you would like to use to make a shadow.

6 After you have shadow pictures of all your animals, turn off the flashlight. Go to a lighted area and mix up the papers. Can you identify each animal by its shadow? What are the clues that help you?

TRY THIS

HAND SHADOW PUPPETS

All you need is a light and your hands to make fun hand shadow puppets. You might even know how to do some already. Try this swan!

Bend your left elbow and wrist. Arch your knuckles on your left hand to make a hook shape that will be the swan's face. Touch your thumb to your index finger leaving a hole for the swan's eye. Open all five fingers on you right hand and put it behind your left elbow to make the swan's feathers.

Check out nomadpress.net/resources for more shadow puppet fun!

TRY THIS

Hearing the Night

Have you ever noticed how noisy it is at night even when you're in a "quiet" place? You might not hear much noise coming from people, but there are plenty of other things to listen to! There are also night sounds you can't even hear. To know what is really going on out there, it helps to know how sounds are made and how ears catch sounds.

If you put your hand on your throat and talk, you'll feel it **vibrate**. These vibrations create **sound waves**. Sound waves can travel through air and water. They can even travel through solids like a wall, table, or the earth!

WORDS TO KNOW

vibrate: to move back and forth very, very quickly.

sound waves: invisible vibrations that you hear as sound.

wavelength: the spacing of sound waves. It is measured by the distance from the high point of one wave to the high point of the next wave.

frequency: the number of sound waves that pass a specific point each second.

Sound waves come in different sizes, or **wavelengths**. When the distance between the waves is short, the sound we hear is higher. When the distance is long, the sound we hear is lower.

DID YOU KNOW?

Sound moves four times faster through water than through air. It can travel such long distances in water that whales can hear each other as far as 100 miles apart (160 kilometers).

Different animals make and hear sound waves of different wavelengths. Bats and insects make very short sound waves. These high-**frequency** waves make sounds that are too high for people to hear. Elephants and whales make large, low-frequency sound waves. These sound waves make sounds that are too deep for us to hear. Humans make sound waves that are somewhere in the middle.

Just for FUN!

I HAVE A FRIEND THAT THINKS SHE IS AN OWL.

Who?

MAKE THAT TWO FRIENDS!

HOW EARS WORK

How well you hear depends a lot on the way you hear. What you see on the sides of your head is part of your outer ear. But most parts of your ears are inside your head. That is where you find the **eardrum**, three tiny bones of the middle ear, and some coiled tubes filled with liquid in the inner ear.

The eardrum is a thin flap of skin that is stretched tight like a drum. When sound waves go through your outer ear and hit the eardrum, the eardrum vibrates. These vibrations move the three tiny bones, which pass on the vibrations to the liquid in the inner ear tubes. These motions hit the **nerves** that send information to your brain. Your brain puts this information together as sound and that's how you hear it!

Most mammals have ears with **pinnae**. A pinna is that funny-shaped piece of skin and **cartilage** you call your ear. A pinna is used to catch sound waves. Dogs, cats, horses, mice, bats, and elephants all have two ears with pinnae.

WORDS ⓣⓞ KNOW

eardrum: a tight flap of skin that separates the middle ear from the outer ear.

nerve: a group of cells bundled together like a wire that sends messages to the brain.

pinna: the skin and cartilage that collects sound waves around the ear. Humans have two pinnae.

cartilage: the stiff, flexible parts of the nose and ear.

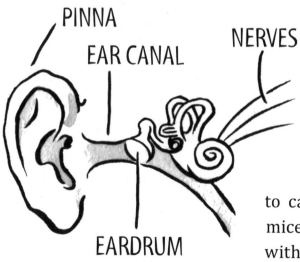

PINNA
EAR CANAL
NERVES
EARDRUM

Some animals, like birds and seals, just have holes on the sides of their heads. Other animals, like frogs, lizards, and insects, have their eardrums right on top of the skin. And some animals, like snakes, do not have any **external** ears at all.

The pinna on each ear collects sound waves and sends them down the ear canal. If a sound is coming from behind you, your pinnae block the waves. You have to turn your head to hear the sound better. Many animals can move each pinna. A cat can turn each ear in a half circle, without moving its head. A rabbit can turn each ear almost three-quarters of a circle.

WORDS TO KNOW

external: on the outside.

DID YOU KNOW?

When you want to hear something better, turn your head toward the sound. Cup a hand behind each ear. This will make your pinnae bigger and make more space to catch sound waves.

HEARING AIDS THROUGH THE AGES

There are many types of natural and man-made hearing aids to help people and animals hear better. Owls can move the circles of feathers on their faces to bring sound to their ears. Bull moose have antlers that move sounds down to their ears. And people have been making hearing aids since prehistoric times. The first hearing aids were hollowed-out cow or ram horns. Later, people used seashells, gold and silver, and other animal horns to make cones they called ear trumpets. Ear trumpets were so popular in the 1800s that they became a fashion statement, like jewelry or cell phones today.

NOCTURNAL ANIMALS NEED TO HEAR

Most animals have very good hearing. Their ears are always moving, trying to catch every sound. Animals need their good hearing for survival. They use it to find food, to avoid getting eaten, and to find each other.

WORDS TO KNOW

echolocation: finding things by sending out sound waves and listening for them to bounce back.

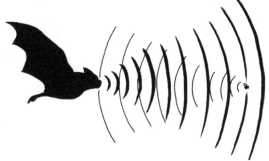

Bats are nocturnal animals that are famous for the way they use their ears. There are over 1,200 different kinds of bats in the world. Some bats eat fruit. Some eat nectar. And a few drink blood. Each of these bats has its own way of finding food. Bats that eat bugs find their dinner by using their ears.

An insect-eating bat makes a lot of high-frequency squeaks as it flies around. The sound waves go out into the air and when they hit something, they bounce off it. Some of these waves bounce back to the bat's ears. This bouncing back and forth is called **echolocation**. The bat hears those sounds and flies toward them, squeaking and listening until it flies right into its dinner!

DID YOU KNOW?

Pallas's long-tongued bats drink plant nectar. Some plants in Cuba have leaves with special shapes. The leaves act like satellite dishes. When the bat makes a sound near the plant, the sound bounces off the leaves and back to the bat's ears. That helps the bat find the plant.

SONAR

Another version of echolocation is called sonar. Sonar stands for **So**und **N**avigation **a**nd **R**anging. Sonar is most often used to find things under water. Dolphins and whales use sonar much more than sight to find food and to navigate. But people also use sonar. As early as 1490, Leonardo da Vinci wrote about listening for underwater sounds. He suggested sticking one end of a tube under water and the other in your ear to hear far-away ships. Over 400 years later, scientists started sending out sound waves under water. Electronic "ears" listen for any sound waves that bounce back. The number and speed of the waves bouncing back help users tell how far away something is, how fast it's moving, and in what direction. The military has used sonar to look for submarines and to map the bottom of the ocean.

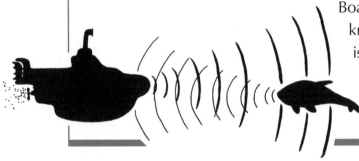

Boats and ships use sonar so they know how deep the water is and to move safely without hitting anything hidden under the surface.

While some bats use sound to find their food, all bats use sounds to talk to each other. Most of the sounds they make are too high pitched for us to hear. But many other nocturnal animals make sounds we can hear. Male animals often call when they are looking for a mate. Parents and young animals call to each other. Animals warn others not to enter their home space by using sounds. Once you learn the animal sounds around you, you'll know what's out there by just using your ears!

CLEVER MOTHS

Some moths have special hearing cells and "ears" that let them hear the sounds that bats make. The moths can then try to trick the bat. When a hawk moth hears a low sound from a bat, it spirals up or just flies away. If the moth hears high-pitched sounds, it knows the bat is getting near. That's when the moth might "drop dead" and fall right down to the ground. Tiger moths confuse bats by sending out their own signals that bats can hear. Underwing moths can make their ears more sensitive to a bat's sound as the bat gets closer. Then, when the bat gets very close, the moth does a power dive to get away.

NIGHT SOUNDS

Most nocturnal animals make sounds at different times in the year. Crickets can be heard at dusk during the summer. Some owls call a lot at dusk in the fall and winter. Frogs sing at dusk in early spring. Coyotes seem to wait until it is dark before they start to yip and yowl. Whip-poor-wills are a country bird active at night. They seem to call their name all night long from mid-spring to late summer.

CHIRP CHIRP
CHIRP
CHIRP

The animal sounds you hear at night depend on where you live. You won't hear a fox in the city, or a peeper in the desert. Crickets live in cities and in the country. They chirp from summer until the first freeze. They call from basements, garages, behind trash cans, and from under leaves and logs.

Nighthawks also live in cities and in the country. Listen on a summer night for a sound like an airplane bomber and you might see a nighthawk diving toward an insect. The sound comes from the bird's wings as it dives toward its food. To get an idea of a nighthawk's call, hold your nose and say the word "peent."

Many animals that call at night make their sounds again and again and again. The animals that sing the loudest are the boys trying to find a girlfriend. A well-known night singer is the spring peeper. A spring peeper is a small frog about the size of your thumb. The males make a high-pitched "peep." They sing in the early spring to show the girl frogs they would be good dads. The stronger they are, the more peeps they make. Some frogs can peep around 4,000 times in one hour. That's more than one peep every second! And they sing all night long!

BE A PEEPER

TRY THIS

Set a timer for 60 seconds on a microwave. Make a high-pitched "peep" sound every second for one minute. If that's too easy, try to peep once every second for five minutes. Imagine doing it for hours and hours without stopping!

TRY THIS

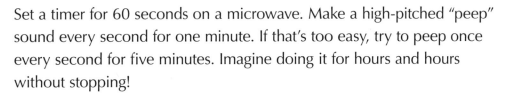

ACTIVITY: **Who Who Hoot Hoot**

What sounds do owls make? Some owls hoot. Other owls beep, click, shriek, or whinny. Even the owls that hoot have different sounds and rhythms. A long-eared owl makes single raspy hoots. A barred owl usually hoots in a pattern of four short hoots, then four short hoots and one long low hoot.

1 Pour water into each bottle until it is about 1 inch deep (2½ centimeters).

2 Pucker your lips like you are going to give a kiss. Put your lips next to the rim of one of the bottles. Do not cover the opening. Blow air across the top. Practice until you get a sound like a hoot.

3 Repeat this over each bottle. Notice the different sounds. Add more water or pour some out.

4 Listen for owls calling outside, even in city parks. Try to match the sounds they make. If you make a sound that is very similar, a real owl might fly over to check you out!

5 Record your owl sounds, then listen to them and experiment to make them even better.

WHOOOOOOoo ?

ACTIVITY: **Frog Song**

It is much easier to hear frogs at night than it is to see them. Male frogs sing from dusk until dawn. Listen for them from early spring through the summer. This is when there is likely to be water in ponds and puddles. Frogs and toads need watery places to lay their eggs. Remember to record when you hear each frog on your night watch.

SUPPLIES

- ✧ paper cup
- ✧ pencil
- ✧ wide rubber band
- ✧ scissors
- ✧ paper clip
- ✧ 2 marbles
- ✧ recording device such as a smartphone or computer program with microphone

1 Use the pencil to poke a hole in the bottom of the paper cup.

2 Cut the rubber band so it is in one long piece. Poke one end through the hole in the cup.

3 Turn the cup upside down. Tie the end of the rubber band to a paper clip. The paper clip should be on the outside of the cup.

4 Hold the cup upside down with one hand. Use your other hand to stretch the rubber band. Wet your thumb. Rub it along the stretched rubber band. It will sound like a pickerel frog. Listen for pickerel frogs from late April through June.

5 Now hold one marble between the thumb and first finger of each hand. Click the marbles together quickly. This is what cricket frogs sound like. Listen for cricket frogs from May to July.

6 Record your frog sounds, and enjoy listening to your "pickerel frogs" and "cricket frogs."

35

ACTIVITY: **Singing Katydids**

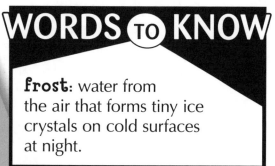

Katydids and cicadas are two of the noisiest insect singers. Listen for them singing in trees from late June until the first **frost**. It is easier to hear a katydid than to see one. They live in forests or fields with lots of shrubs or trees. They are brown or green and their wings look like leaves. During late summer, they make a chhhhh-chhhhh-chhhhh sound by rubbing the edges of their two front wings together. One wing edge has teeth like a comb. The other wing edge is like a stick that scrapes the teeth.

WORDS TO KNOW

frost: water from the air that forms tiny ice crystals on cold surfaces at night.

1 Hold the comb with the teeth pointing up.

2 Rub the stick quickly back and forth on top of the teeth.

3 Record the sound of your katydid.

Just for FUN!

WHAT GAME DO KATYDIDS LIKE TO PLAY MOST?

Cricket!

ACTIVITY: **Singing Cicadas**

Cicadas spend part of their lives underground. They crawl around and poke holes in tree roots to get a drink of sap. When it is summer, young cicadas come above ground. The back of their hard shell splits open. An adult cicada with wings climbs out. They spread their wings and fly up into a tree. In the late afternoon from June through September, male cicadas start to sing. They do this by pushing a special skin, called the tymbal, in and out on the sides of their bodies. They sing until dark.

1 Place the metal lid on a table. Push the button in the middle of the lid down. Let it pop up.

2 Push the button down and up as fast as you can to hear the sounds of the cicada.

3 Record the sound of your cicada.

DID YOU KNOW?

Cicadas can bend their tymbal up and down 50 times each second!

TRY THIS

MAKE A NIGHT CHORUS

Once you've recorded your owl, frog, katydid, and cicada sounds, see if your family and friends can guess what they are. Teach them to make the sounds and then play them all together in a dark room to have a true night chorus! You can also try to make a music recording of all the different sounds.

TRY THIS

ACTIVITY: **Here's to Ears!**

Find out two reasons why many animals have better hearing than humans.

1 Go to a place where you can turn on a radio and TV, and open the windows so there is a lot of noise.

2 Cut one long strip off each piece of paper. Tape the two strips together to make one long strip. Put the rest of the paper aside for now.

3 Wrap the strip of paper around your head so it goes over both your ears and tape it.

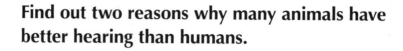

4 Close your eyes. Turn around slowly in a circle three times. With your eyes closed, say the name of one noise source and point to it with one hand. Keep your eyes closed and name another source and point to it with your other hand. Open your eyes. Did you point right at the noisemakers?

Just for FUN!

WHAT SECRET DID ONE EAR TELL THE OTHER?

Between us, we have brains!

5 Take the two leftover pieces of paper and roll each one into a cone shape. Make sure to leave a 1-inch opening at the top of each cone (2½ centimeters). The other side should be as wide as possible. Tape the edge so the cones keep their shape.

6 Make sure it is still noisy. Close your eyes. Spin around three times. With your eyes closed, put the smaller end of each cone near an ear. Move the cones up and down. How do they change your hearing?

CLASSROOM CONNECTION: Ask your teacher to try this experiment in the classroom. Your classmates should be able to make plenty of noise to add to other noise sources. Have each student make their own ear cones in all different sizes. Keep track of how many kids identified the sounds correctly and how many did not. What was the biggest challenge? Did the size of the cones make a difference in the student's ability to identify sounds? What are the reasons some animals often have better hearing than humans?

EQUAL EARS

Our ears are usually in about the same place on each side of the head. But most owls have ears at different levels. The saw-whet owl's right ear is up high and its left ear is down low. Sounds from below the owl reach the left ear first and sounds from above the owl reach the right ear first. This helps the owl hunt even when it can't see very well.

ACTIVITY: **Yardstick Sound**

SUPPLIES

✧ yardstick
✧ table

Anything that moves the air around it makes a sound. Sounds are airwaves that your ear can detect.

1 Place a yardstick flat on a table. Slide about 4 inches of the yardstick over the edge of the table (10 centimeters). Use one hand to hold the yardstick on the table so it doesn't move.

2 Press the thumb of your other hand on the end of the yardstick still on the table. Slide your thumb along the yardstick and then past the overhanging edge. Watch and listen to the sound the yardstick makes. Is the sound high or low? Does it make a low-frequency or high-frequency sound? Do you think the sound waves were short or long?

3 Now move the yardstick so that 20 inches hang over the edge (50 centimeters). Watch and listen as you push down with your thumb and slide it past the free edge again. Did the end of the stick move slower or faster than the first time? Were its movements bigger or shorter? Was it a lower-pitched or a higher-pitched sound? Do you think the sound waves were low frequency or high frequency?

4 Move the yardstick even more, so that 32 inches hang over the edge (80 centimeters). Watch and listen as you push and release the free edge again. Are you able to hear the sound it makes?

ACTIVITY: **Bat and Bug**

Most bats are not really blind, but the people playing the bat in this game will be. It will test their ability to echolocate!

1 Use the rope to make a circle on the ground. This is the cave the bat and bug are in.

2 Each person gets two sticks. One person is the bat. The bat puts on the blindfold and spins around three times. While the bat is spinning, the person playing the bug picks a place to stand in the cave.

3 When the bat stops spinning, he or she taps the two sticks together. Every time the bat clicks the sticks, the bug has to click his or her sticks as an echo. The bat then walks toward the sound. The bug cannot move to another spot, but can tap the sticks up high, down low, or to the side.

4 The bat keeps clicking the sticks until he or she tags the bug. After the bug has been caught, switch roles and play again.

5 For more fun, play the game again with the bug being able to move around anywhere inside the cave during the game.

Smelling the Night

Smell is a very important sense for most animals, especially at night. Sometimes an animal doesn't want to be seen or heard. But all animals need to **communicate** with other animals. Sometimes they need to keep in touch with members of their family so they can stay together. Other times, they need to tell certain animals to stay away. But if they want to be silent and invisible, how do they communicate? They use smells!

WORDS TO KNOW

communicate: to share information in some way, such as sounds, words, or actions.

42

How do animals make smells? Animals have many **glands** in their bodies. Glands are little sacs inside an animal's body. Each type of gland has a special job. There are glands to make your spit, tears, sweat, and many other things your body needs. And then there are the smell-making glands.

CAN YOU SMELL THAT?

Have you ever seen a cat rubbing its face against something? It was rubbing a smell on it from the glands on its face. Deer have smell-making glands on their legs and between their toes. People have smell-making glands in their armpits. Skunks and their relatives, including weasels, otters, and ferrets, have smell-making glands under their tails.

Many animals can make more than one kind of smell. Animals make some smells to mark their homes. These smells are often found in their pee and poop. These smells are heavy and don't move very far. They make other smells to find each other. When an animal uses its smell to find a mate, it makes a light smell that can float in the air. This helps animals find each other even when they are far apart. Skunks and some snakes make strong smells to keep other animals from eating them.

Just for FUN!

HOW DO YOU MAKE A SKUNK STOP SMELLING?

Plug up its nose!

SNIFF
SNIFF

WORDS (TO) KNOW

chemical: a substance that has certain features that can react with other substances.

antenna: one of two moveable feelers on an insect's head that it uses mainly for smelling. It can also be used for sensing touch, heat, sound, and taste. Plural is antennae.

Most mammals use their noses to smell. The **chemicals** that make up the smells go to special cells high in the nose. These cells send signals to the part of the brain that identifies smells. Some animals, like snakes and elephants, have special smelling areas in the top of their mouths too.

Animals with longer, wetter noses have a better sense of smell than mammals with short, dry noses. Long noses give more room for special smelling cells. Some dogs are 10 million times better at smelling than humans! This doesn't mean they smell 10 million things we can't. It means they need a lot less of a smell to notice it.

Insects use their **antennae** or feet for smelling. Some moths have huge antennae that look like big feathers. These antennae make moths extra sensitive to certain smells. Female silkworm moths make a special smell so the males can find them. A male silkworm moth can notice that smell from over 6 miles away (9½ kilometers).

Even though humans do not have the best sense of smell, our noses can still recognize around 10,000 different scents. And you can teach your nose to work even better.

How do you teach a nose new tricks? The more you use your sense of smell, the better it will become. Every day, smell your bath towel. Smell your socks. Smell your mittens. Smell the carpet. Smell a piece of bread. Smell a flower, soil, and water. Smell your food. Smell your drinks. Sniff at night and sniff during the day. Smells seem stronger at night than they do during the day. This is mainly because you can't rely on your eyes, so you start paying more attention to your other senses.

DID YOU KNOW?

Scientists have discovered that Asian elephants and 140 kinds of moths use one of the same smells to communicate!

TRY THIS

WET SNIFFER TEST

There's another reason your sense of smell works better at night. Water doesn't just make your nose wet, it actually helps your sense of smell work better! And at night the air often has more moisture in it.

* Go outside and sniff the air around you. Then, go back inside and drink some water. With your mouth closed, go outside again and breathe deeply through your nose. See if you notice more smells than before.

* Pour a spice like basil or cinnamon in one hand. Sniff it. Dip a finger in water and rub the end of your nose. Sniff the spice again. Fill a cup with the hottest water you can get from your tap. Put your nose over it, breathe in, and then sniff the spice again. Which time did the spice smell the strongest?

SMELL BUSTERS

There are times when you don't want to smell nocturnal animals, and you don't want them to smell you either. For example, mosquitoes use your smell as a clue to find you. To keep from getting bitten, you might put on bug spray. Bug sprays are mixtures of different chemicals. Some bug sprays work by trying to cover your natural smells. Other bug sprays work by clogging up mosquitoes' smelling cells.

These sprays are not perfect. They don't seem to work for some people. Some people don't like how the spray feels or smells. After a few hours, the sprays wear off and don't work anymore. And you shouldn't use these sprays on your hands right before you try to catch frogs, toads, or salamanders. These animals breathe through their skin, so they are very sensitive to chemicals.

DID YOU KNOW?

Only female mosquitoes suck your blood. They need blood as food for laying eggs. Male mosquitoes feed on flower nectar.

Some people are lucky. Mosquitoes don't seem to like how they smell. Scientists asked some of these people to sleep in special smell-collecting bags. Then the scientists worked to make and test the chemicals they found. They hope to make bug sprays that are safer, smell better, and work longer than the ones we use today.

Until the new sprays are ready, here are some tricks to getting fewer mosquito bites without using chemicals.

✳ Wear light-colored clothes.

✳ Try not to go out at dusk or dawn in the summer. This is when mosquitoes are most active.

✳ Be still. Mosquitoes can sense body heat, sweat, and carbon dioxide. All of these increase if you are moving around a lot.

SKUNK AWAY

There is another smelly secret that is good to know. What should you do if you get sprayed by a skunk? For many years, people bathed their sprayed pets in tomato juice to try to get rid of the smell, but it didn't help very much. Then a scientist discovered a new smell-busting recipe. It works much better and uses items you can find in most grocery stores. Don't make this mixture until you need it. And don't try to store it in a bottle. It makes a lot of bubbles that can cause a bottle to pop open.

In a large bowl, mix together 1 quart of 3% hydrogen peroxide, ¼ cup baking soda, and 2 teaspoons of liquid dish detergent. The mixture will start foaming. Cover the stinky surface with the suds. Leave the suds on for five minutes, then rinse them off with clean water.

We aren't the only ones trying to confuse other animals' sense of smell. **Predators** like wolves will roll in the poop of the animals they want to eat. That way the wolves can sneak up closer without their smell giving them away. **Prey** use the same trick. Some ground squirrels rub themselves with snake skin. This makes snakes more likely to leave them alone. Instead of trying to trick predators with a different scent, a baby deer has no scent at all. When a baby deer is lying still, it is very hard for a predator to find it.

DID YOU KNOW?

Great horned owls are one of the few animals that will eat a skunk! The owl's eyes take up so much room in its head that there is no room left for a sense of smell.

ENJOY THE SMELL OF THE NIGHT

Get outside at night in all the seasons to enjoy the smells. Take a deep breath through your nose. Your sense of smell is sharpened in the dark.

A great way to enjoy night smells in the summer and attract moths is to plant a night garden. Some plants open only at night. These plants are usually white so they are easy to see. Many night-blooming plants have strong smells. This makes it easier for moths and bats to find them in the dark.

ACTIVITY: **Moth Bait**

Moths use their excellent sense of smell to find food and each other. Food for most moths is flower nectar, plant sap, or the juices from rotting fruit. That makes it easy to mix up a batch of smelly moth food. Use it to attract moths to your area.

1 Peel the banana and put it in the plastic tub. Mash it with the spoon. Add five spoonfuls of fruit juice, two spoonfuls of sugar, and one spoonful of molasses. Stir it all together. Put the lid on the tub. Set it in a warm place for two days or more. You want it to be very smelly.

2 Just before it gets dark, take the tub of moth bait and the paintbrush outside. Dip the brush into the goo. Dab it about chest high onto the side of a tree or pole. Rough surfaces that have cracks to hold the goo work best. Make goo patches about 5 inches square (12½ centimeters). Do a couple trees or poles close to each other. When you are done, leave the area.

3 About 15 minutes after dark, quietly sneak up on the bait spots. Keep your flashlight off until you are right next to a painted patch. Keep your flashlight below the patch. Turn it on and shine it upwards. If there aren't any moths, visit your next patch.

4 Paint the trees and poles with moth bait several times during the summer. Which trees get the most moths? Do you attract more moths in the summer or the fall? How many different types of moths do you see? Mark your results on your night watch.

SUPPLIES

- ✧ overripe banana
- ✧ plastic tub with lid
- ✧ spoon
- ✧ fruit juice
- ✧ sugar
- ✧ molasses
- ✧ wide paintbrush

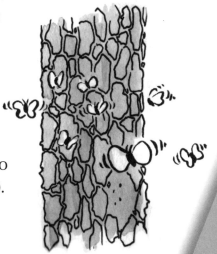

ACTIVITY: **Night Garden**

If you live where it is always warm, you might get night bloomers all year long. If you live where it gets cold in the winter, enjoy a night garden in the summer.

1 Look at the chart on the next page to find a plant that will fit in your tub or flowerpot. The easiest time to get seeds or young plants is in the spring.

2 If you are using a plastic tub, poke a few holes in the bottom. Fill your tub or pot with soil.

3 Follow the instructions on your seed packet or plant label. Remember, even though these plants bloom at night, they need sunlight during the day to grow. Water your plants when they are dry.

4 If you can, keep the plants outside. Once they bloom, watch the plants to see if they get any night visitors.

5 When a plant is blooming, try to trick it. Take it to a dark closet or room during the day. Does a blossom open? Shine a bright light on the plant at night. Does the blossom close?

PLANT	DESCRIPTION	CARE	TYPE AND SIZE
Moonflower	Big white blooms that open at night. Smells a bit lemony.	Full sun. Drought resistant.	Not good in small pots. Likes to spread out or climb. Needs lots of room.
Evening Primrose "Sundrops"	Big yellow blooms.	Full sun. No special care.	Easy to grow. Can be in medium pots. Will grow back every year.
Night Phlox "Midnight Candy"	Small white blooms. Very strong smell.	Full sun. Low water.	Easy to grow. Can be in small to medium pots or in the garden.
Evening Stock "Night Violets"	Small purple flower. Strong smell.	Sun to part shade. Likes cool weather.	Good for everything from small pots to garden edges.

CLASSROOM CONNECTION: Take pictures of your night garden during the day, at night, and whenever you see a night visitor. Share the photos with your classmates. Bring in one of your night-blooming plants and have your classmates shine a light on it in a dark place so they can watch it bloom before they eyes.

ACTIVITY: **Spreading Smells**

Use tea bags to discover how animals can spread their smells the farthest. Ask an adult to prepare and pour the hot water.

1 In your journal, use the ruler and pencil to make a chart with three columns and four rows. Label the second column Bright and the third column Dark. In the first column, starting with the second row, label the rows Dry, Warm, and Blowing.

	BRIGHT	DARK
Dry		
Warm		
Blowing		

2 Smell the dry tea bags. Place one in each of the cups. Place one cup in a well-lighted area, a second cup in a dark area, and the third cup in the refrigerator. Move away from all of the cups for five minutes.

3 Put the small tokens in your hand or pocket. Go back to the bright area where you put the first cup. Start walking toward the cup and place a token on the ground as soon as you smell the tea. Measure the distance from the cup to the token. Record the result in your journal. Do the same with the second cup in the dark room.

4 Ask an adult to pour about 3 inches of very hot water onto the tea bags in the first two cups (7½ centimeters). Take the third cup out of the fridge. Pour about 3 inches of cold water onto this tea bag (7½ centimeters).

5 Watch how the color spreads through the water. This is also spreading the taste and smell of the tea. Does the tea move faster through hot water or cold water? Put the first two cups back in their light and dark areas. Move away again for five minutes.

6 Walk back towards the first cup and place a token on the floor as soon as you smell the tea. Measure the distance from the cup to the token. Do the same for the second cup. Record the results in your journal.

7 Place the fans so each is blowing over a cup with tea and warm water. Leave for 5 minutes.

8 Go back and again place a token on the floor as soon as you smell the tea in each cup. Measure the distance from the cup to the tokens. Record the results in your journal.

9 Look at your journal results. Did you smell the tea from farther away in the dark area or in the bright area? Why? Would an animal smell travel farther in warm air or in cold air? In calm air or in the wind?

Feeling the Night

What does it mean to "feel" the night? It doesn't mean your mood—like happy or excited. It means to pay attention to what your skin is telling you. Your skin is the largest **organ** in your body. It weighs between 6 and 10 pounds (3 to 4½ kilograms).

WORDS (TO) KNOW

organ: a part of the body with a special function, like the heart, lungs, brain, and skin.

Most of the time, you ignore much of what you feel. You don't really feel the clothes you are wearing, unless they are too tight or scratchy. You don't notice if the air is dry or moist unless it's raining.

Night scientists need to collect information from all their senses. Your skin can tell you about things your eyes, ears, nose, and mouth can't. You can't hear how warm it is outside. You can't taste if the ground is smooth. You need your sense of touch.

Your sense of touch works because of nerves. These are thin threads of special cells called **neurons**. Sensory neurons are the ones used to give you a sense of touch. There are sensory neurons under your skin everywhere on your body.

When you touch something, the sensory neuron at that spot starts a chemical and electrical message that travels from nerve to nerve until it gets to your brain. Your brain takes the information and uses it to help you identify things. Your brain can also use that information to send messages to your muscles. If you are touching something hot that might burn you, your brain will say, "move away!"

PINS AND NEEDLES

Have you ever had a hand or foot "fall asleep?" This tingling feeling comes after you put pressure on an area for a long time. When you do this, you are pinching the lines of nerves so they can't send messages to your brain. Your brain can't send messages to your nerves or your muscles. When you finally let up on the pressure, the nerves rush to get working again. They quickly send a bunch of messages to the brain to say they are on. These quick messages coming all at once create the funny feeling of pins and needles.

There are four main types of touches. Your skin can tell you about hot, cold, pain, and pressure. By combining these, your brain can also feel if something is hard, soft, silky, scratchy, wet, or dry. Have you ever felt a fly land on your arm before you saw it? Or a horse's warm breath on your neck? Maybe while walking down a dark trail, you've run into a spider's web and felt its sticky threads. You can use your sense of touch to tell winter is almost over when you feel an icicle drip on your hair. Your sensory nerves are hard at work, day and night!

FEELING BETTER

In addition to their skin, most nocturnal animals have extra feelers on their bodies. Katydids, lightning beetles, and other insects use their antennae on the top of their heads. Owls and night hawks have thin, hair-like feathers near their beaks.

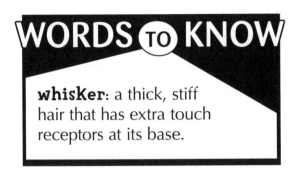

whisker: a thick, stiff hair that has extra touch receptors at its base.

Most mammals have extra-long, thick hairs called **whiskers** around their mouths and noses. Flying squirrels have whiskers around their mouths, eyes, and their front paws. Some bats even have whiskers on their rumps!

Extra feelers, whether they are whiskers or antennae, are very sensitive to air movements. A moving feeler tells an animal that it is close to something, or that something is moving, even if it can't be seen. Rats, opossums, and flying squirrels move their whiskers to help them identify the shape and size of things. Their whiskers are so sensitive, they're almost like another set of fingers!

DID YOU KNOW?

Some people call the hairs growing around a man's mouth and on his cheeks and neck whiskers. Although all the hairs on humans have sensory neurons at their base, a man's facial hair isn't nearly as sensitive as the whiskers on many animals.

Why do animals need these extra feelers? Imagine you are crawling through a dark room. If your hands and feet are on the floor, the first part of your body to touch a chair or wall will be your head. Ouch! An extra set of feelers would let you feel in front and to your sides so you wouldn't bump into anything.

FEEL THE HUMIDITY

WORDS TO KNOW

humidity: the amount of water in the air.

When you go outside at night, you may notice that it feels damp. That's because of increased **humidity**. Low humidity means there is very little water in the air. This is true most of the time in a desert. High humidity means there is a lot of water in the air. This is true in a rainforest. The amount of water that the air can hold depends on the temperature of the air. Hot air can hold more water than cold air. At night, the air cools down. When it cools, it releases water and the air feels more humid.

WORDS TO KNOW

condensation: when water vapor sticks together to make droplets.

dew: water droplets made when humid air cools at night.

This water vapor that the air lets out can stick together. It forms droplets on grass, leaves, cars, and other cool things. These droplets are called **condensation**. The condensation that happens when humid air cools during the night is called **dew**. If the night air is very cold, the tiny water droplets will form ice crystals. This is called frost.

FEEL THE HEAT

TRY THIS

Get five pennies from different years. Put four of the pennies in a bag. Look at the date on the fifth penny. Hold that penny in a fist for two minutes. Drop the penny into the bag. Shake the bag three times. Reach your hand in the bag. Pull out the penny that feels the warmest. Is it the one you were holding in your fist? **Helpful Hint:** Rubbing your hands together and giving each fingertip a gentle pinch will give your fingertips a better sense of touch.

COOLING DOWN

Most of the time, the earth cools down at night. This is okay for most furry and feathery animals. Mammals and birds have bodies that can make heat. They are warm-blooded. Their coats keep that heat close to their bodies.

But amphibians and reptiles don't make their own heat. They have no coats and they do not have a built-in way to stay warm. They are cold-blooded. So to keep warm, they find the warmest place they can.

Just for FUN!

WHAT DO REPTILES WEAR TO KEEP WARM?

Turtlenecks!

HEAT PITS

Vipers, boas, and pythons are all snakes that have heat-detecting pits on their heads. The cells in these pits can detect a difference in temperature of much less than one degree Celsius or Fahrenheit. This helps a snake tell if a warm-blooded animal is near. For a long time, scientists thought snakes were the only animals with backbones that could do that. That was until a team studying vampire bats found heat-detecting cells on their faces too.

HEAT PITS

Some things hold heat better than others. At dusk after a sunny
day, feel a sidewalk or rock that has been in the sun. Feel the
grass or a plant. If you were an animal trying to be warm, which
one would you lie on?

In the country, the warmest place to be is often on a paved
road. On cool summer nights, look for frogs, toads, snakes, and
turtles sitting on warm roads. Many cities have plenty of stone
and brick buildings. These buildings help keep the city warmer
at night. In the winter, crows and other birds will flock to cities
to keep warm.

ACTIVITY: **Touch Test**

SUPPLIES

- 2 bags (paper sacks or pillow cases)
- 2 large marbles
- 2 small marbles
- 2 matching bottle caps
- 2 matching milk jug caps
- 2 dimes
- 2 nickels
- 2 pennies
- 2 small paper clips
- 2 large paper clips
- bowl of hot water
- bowl of cold water
- liquid soap
- sandpaper

How good is your sense of touch? Can anything make it better or worse?

1 One bag is for your right hand. The other bag is for your left hand. Put one of each of the small items into each bag.

2 Once your bags are filled, start testing yourself. But don't peek! First see if you can pull the small paper clip out of each bag. Next, pull out the large marbles. Did you get the right things?

3 Put everything back in its bag. Dip one hand in the bowl of hot water. Dip the other hand in the cold water. Leave them in the water as you count to 100. Take your hands out and place one in each bag. Take out the large paper clips. Find the nickels. Was it easier to find the items with your warm hand or your cold hand?

4 Put everything back in its bag. Spread some liquid soap on the fingers of your right hand. If you got any soap on your left hand, wash it off. Gently rub the fingers of your left hand on the sandpaper. Then reach into each bag for the two bottle caps. Find the dimes. Was it easier to find the items with your smooth hand or your rough hand?

ACTIVITY: **Dew It!**

You can see water condense when you chill a jar of hot, humid air. Ask an adult to heat and pour the water for you.

1 Fill the jar with very hot water. Count to 60. While you are counting, put 10 large ice cubes in a plastic bag.

2 Pour out the water until there is only 1 inch of it left in the bottom (2½ centimeters). Notice how the jar looks clear.

3 Put the bag of ice so it sits over the top of the jar. Watch what happens as the warm air gets cooled down.

4 Put the black paper behind the jar. Shine the flashlight through the jar onto the paper. What do you see?

SUPPLIES

✧ clear plastic jar
✧ hot water
✧ 10 ice cubes
✧ thin plastic bag
✧ black paper
✧ flashlight

DID YOU KNOW?

A ring around the moon is made from light bouncing through tiny ice crystals high in the atmosphere.

63

Night Lights

A clear night is never totally dark. There are lots of things that make light, like stars, fireflies, streetlights, and car lights. There are things that reflect light, like the moon, planets, animal eyes, and street signs. What type of night lights do you see?

DID YOU KNOW?

If you want the best possible night vision in a dark place, cover your flashlight lens with a piece of red cellophane.

STREETLIGHTS

Before there were streetlights, people carried torches or lanterns at night. Some of the first street lamps in the United States were candles on top of tall posts. These candles had four pieces of glass around them so the wind couldn't blow them out.

Inventors have worked to make streetlights better ever since. They created lights that used gas and later electricity, instead of candles or oil. They made lights that could turn on with a switch and shine the light in a certain direction. Some lights use sensors that make them turn on when it starts to get dark and turn off when it starts to get light again.

Streetlights make people feel safer. They help us find our way and see nocturnal animals that are close by. Having some light at night is useful. But too much light at night can be a problem.

DID YOU KNOW?

Most people use flashlights the wrong way. If you hold it in front of you, you will only pay attention to what is in the circle of light. But if you hold it up next to your eyes, it shines where your eyes are looking. This will help you see the eye shine of animals better as well.

Too much light at night makes it hard to study the stars and planets. When there are too many lights, night-blooming plants open their flowers later. Moths fly in circles around lights instead of finding food or mates. Some frogs won't sing if there is too much light. Most people don't sleep as well if there is too much light.

WORDS TO KNOW

light pollution: too much man-made light during the night from street lights, signs, and buildings, so that it is hard to see stars. Plants and animals can act differently when there is too much light at night.

Too much light at night is called **light pollution**. Newer streetlights still make the light people need and use less energy. They create less light pollution. To measure light pollution, scientists look at how many stars they can see at one time. The more stars they see, the less light pollution there is.

1, 2, 3, 4, 5...

Just for **FUN!**

WHAT DO YOU SEE MORE OF WHEN THERE IS LESS LIGHT?

Darkness.

REFLECTORS

Reflectors throw light in a certain direction. They don't **absorb** light at all. Reflectors are used on streetlights, road signs, road stripes, bikes, clothes, and even dog collars to make them visible at night. If you look closely at some reflectors, you'll usually see diamond patterns. These break up the light source and reflect it back to you.

When you move a flashlight around outside at night, you might see pairs of small reflectors that are moving! Be careful! It might be the reflected eye shine of a nocturnal animal.

WORDS TO KNOW

reflector: a piece of glass, metal, or other material that sends, or reflects, light back.

absorb: to soak up a liquid or take in energy, heat, light, or sound.

tapetum lucidum: a special layer of cells found behind the retina in many animals' eyes. These cells reflect light.

Many nocturnal animals have a special layer of cells behind the retina in their eyes called the **tapetum lucidum**. The tapetum acts like a reflector.

COUNTING CROCODILES

A *National Geographic* wildlife expert named Brady Barr went into a cave in Costa Rica looking for crocodiles. He turned on his flashlight and saw orange crocodile eyes reflecting back at him. When the seven crocodiles in the cave started to growl, Brady's team quickly pulled him out!

The reflected light gives the rod and cone cells in the animal's eyes extra light to work. This helps them see better at night. It also helps us see the animals better! The color of an animal's eye shine is one more clue to help you identify it.

ANIMAL	EYE SHINE COLOR
Opossums & Raccoons	Yellow
Deer	White
Foxes & Rabbits	Red
Cats	Green

MOONSHINE

The brightest natural light you see at night is a natural reflector called the moon. The moon does not make any of its own light. It reflects about 7 percent of the sunlight that hits it. This reflected light is what we see. When the moon is full, it gives about the same amount of light as a bright streetlight.

You've probably looked up at the moon many times. Have you noticed that it seems to change shape? Of course, the moon isn't actually changing shape. Because the moon is always traveling around the earth, we see a different part of it reflected than we did the night before. The lighted part of the moon is facing the sun. The part facing away from the sun is dark.

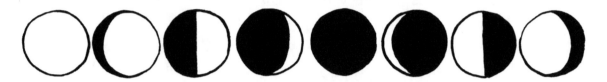

Each "shape" of the moon is a phase that has a name. The phases of the moon depend on where the moon and sun are. Sometimes, when the moon and sun are on the same side of the earth, you cannot see the moon at all. When the moon and sun are on opposite sides of the earth, the moon looks like a big, bright circle. When the moon looks like a half circle, it is called a quarter moon. When the moon looks a bit like a banana, it is called a crescent moon. When the moon looks like a ball that is losing air, it is called a gibbous moon. Can you tell which phase is which from the descriptions?

REFLECTING PLANETS

All the planets, including Earth, reflect light, just like the moon. If they didn't reflect light, we wouldn't be able to see them! Like Earth, all planets orbit the sun. They look like bright stars in the sky. You can often find Venus just by looking for the brightest "star" just before dawn or just after dark.

Everyone sees the same phase of the moon, everywhere on Earth. But there is a difference in what you see that depends on where you are. What if you live in the **Northern Hemisphere** and you see a crescent moon curving left? On the same night, people in the **Southern Hemisphere** will see the crescent moon curving right. If it's a quarter or gibbous moon, and people in the Northern Hemisphere see it facing right, people in the Southern Hemisphere will see it facing left. When there is a full moon though, everyone sees the same thing!

STAR BRIGHT

Most of the stars you see in the night sky are huge fireballs far away. Stars make light by burning gases. Before there was a lot of man-made light, star gazers could see over 2,000 stars at one time in the night sky. This was too many single stars to keep track of! **Astronomers** looked for patterns in the stars. They used the stars to make dot-to-dot pictures of people and animals. We call these pictures **constellations**.

THE STARS ARE FALLING!

One type of star is not on any star map. It is a falling star. Falling stars are not really stars. They are small dusty pieces of **asteroids** or other space material. The pieces get so hot when they go through Earth's atmosphere that they glow as they fall. They make a line of light through the sky. This line of light looks like a star is falling. Scientists call them meteors. The pieces usually burn up before they get all the way to the ground. The pieces that do make it to the ground are called **meteorites**.

> ## WORDS (TO) KNOW
>
> **asteroid:** a small rocky object orbiting the sun. Asteroids are too small to be planets.
>
> **meteorite:** any piece of space material that makes it to the surface of the earth after falling through the atmosphere.

At certain spots in its orbit, Earth goes through places in space where there are a lot of asteroid pieces. This is when you can try to see falling stars. Astronomers call these times meteor showers. The best time to look for falling stars is after midnight. During the biggest meteor showers, you might see around 100 falling stars every hour, if you can stay awake!

Mark these meteor showers on your night watch. If the sky is clear, take some blankets outside. Go to the darkest place you can find, lie on your back, and look up at the sky.

* **Quatrantids** January 2–5
* **Perseids** August 10–13
* **Leonids** November 15–17

Just as the sun appears to rise in the east and set in the west each day, so do the stars. This means that the constellations you see when the sun goes down are in different places than they are at bedtime or just before dawn if you wake up really early. But it's not because the sun and stars are moving in the sky. It's because the earth is spinning all the time. So even though you don't feel the spinning, you are looking up at different spots in the sky at different times.

The earth is also moving around the sun in its orbit. It takes a full year for Earth to orbit the sun. So your view of the stars in the galaxy changes all the time. The group of constellations you see will depend on where the earth is in its orbit. Some constellations are seen in the winter and others only in the summer.

DID YOU KNOW?

Our wobbling Earth has also caused the North Star to change. Over 6,000 years ago, the star closest to the North Pole was Thuban, not Polaris. You can still see Thuban. It is between the Big and Little Dippers as a part of the constellation Draco the Dragon.

GLOW IN THE DARK

Have you ever used a glow stick? There are two tubes. The big plastic one on the outside is filled with one chemical. Another chemical is in a small glass tube in the middle. When you bend the plastic tube, the glass tube breaks. The two chemicals mix together and make light.

WORDS TO KNOW

bioluminescent: when living things give off light.

abdomen: one of three parts of a beetle that is located after its hind legs.

There are a few plants and animals that mix chemicals to make their own light. They are **bioluminescent**. Bio means life and lumen means light. Bioluminescent plants and animals have special chemicals in their bodies that mix together to make light.

One well-known bioluminescent creature is called a firefly, or lightning bug. This insect is actually a beetle. The adult beetles mix the chemicals at the ends of their bodies in their **abdomens**. Most fireflies use their lights to find mates.

73

WORDS (TO) KNOW

fungus: a plant-like living thing without leaves or flowers. It grows on plants and things that are rotting, like old logs. Examples are mold, mildew, and mushrooms. Plural is fungi.

larva: the worm form of an insect. Plural is larvae.

spore: a tiny one-celled living thing produced by fungi. It is like an egg, because it can grow into an adult of the fungus.

Other living things that make their own lights include glowworms, anglerfish, and a **fungus** called foxfire found on rotting trees. Glowworms are the **larvae** of fireflies. Glowworms and anglerfish use their lights so that animals they want to eat will come close. Some scientists think that foxfire makes its own light to warn animals not to eat it. Other scientists think foxfire makes its own light so that insects will land on it. When the insects leave, they spread **spores** from the foxfire that will grow into foxfire in new places.

DID YOU KNOW?

Soldiers tried using glow-in-the-dark foxfire to provide light in a submarine called the Turtle during the Revolutionary War. But when the submarine was underwater, it got too cold for the foxfire to glow.

Just for FUN!

HOW DO FIREFLIES START A RACE?

Ready, set, glow!

ACTIVITY: **Direct the Light**

Old-fashioned streetlights shine a lot of light where it isn't needed. They leave some important areas dark. Newer lights have caps that spread the light and shine it where it is needed. Less light is put into the atmosphere.

SUPPLIES

- ✧ flashlight or lamp
- ✧ white poster board
- ✧ small toy figure
- ✧ metal pie tin

1 If you are using a lamp, remove the shade from the light bulb.

2 Stand the light in the middle of the poster board. The bulb should be facing up.

3 Place the toy about 3 inches away from the base of the light (7½ centimeters).

4 Turn on the light. Turn off all other lights. Look at the shadow under the light. Where is the light going?

5 Hold your hands over, but not touching, the light. What happens to the shadow? Does the board look brighter or darker?

6 Hold the pie tin over the light. What happens to the shadow? Does the board look brighter or darker?

NOTE: Your hands and the pie tin act as reflectors. They direct light down. This means there are fewer dark areas and less light pollution. Look at the streetlights near your home. Do they have reflectors?

ACTIVITY: **Night Light Survey**

A survey is when you look at something carefully and collect information about it. A survey of the lights you see at night will help you find the darkest place where you live. This survey is best done on a clear night.

1 Put the paper on the clipboard and make a chart like the one on the following page.

2 When it gets dark, go outside and stand near your front door. Count how many lights you see of each type. Write this number in each section using one color of pencil. If you are in a very dark place, you might need to guess how many stars you can see.

3 On another evening, go to another place outside. It could be behind your house or in a park. If you live in an apartment that lets you on the roof, ask if you can do your survey there. Use a different color of pencil to record the number of lights you see of each kind.

4 Do this in as many places as you can. Look at your chart. Compare how many stars you see in the each place. Can you see colors? Can you see shapes? Which place would you say is the darkest? Which is the lightest?

5 You can get up early and do the same experiment just before dawn. If you do, add another column to your chart called, "Before dawn, I see . . . "

6 Use this chart to help you decide when and where to do night science. If you want to see stars, pick a night that does not have a lot of moonlight and go to a place without many other lights. If you want to see moths flying (and maybe bats and nighthawks!), look around powerful lights that are up high, like those above a parking lot or sports field.

		AFTER DUSK, I SEE . . .
NATURAL LIGHT	**Stars**	
	Moon	
	Fireflies	
	Fire	
	Other natural light (snow)	
MAN-MADE LIGHT	**Street lights**	
	Porch lights	
	Window lights	
	Car lights (headlights, tail lights, police lights, etc.)	
	Neon lights, lighted signs	
	Safety lights (traffic signals, construction markers)	
	Flashlights	
	Other man-made light	

ACTIVITY: **Marshmallow Moons**

SUPPLIES

✧ 5 large marshmallows

✧ bamboo skewer

✧ lump of clay

✧ 5 tables or boxes (all the same height)

✧ 4 sticky notes or index cards

✧ pencil

✧ lamp or flashlight

Do not mark moon phases on your night watch. The dates will change every year. Instead, you're going to take a bite out of the moon!

1 Poke one marshmallow onto one end of the skewer and put the other end of the skewer into the lump of clay. This will keep your moon standing up.

2 Set up 4 tables or boxes in a square. There should be a space in the middle big enough for you to stand in and turn around.

3 Label the 4 sticky notes or index cards 1–4. Place one on each table going around clockwise to the right. Then put a marshmallow on each table.

4 Put the fifth table outside the square across from Table 1. Stand the light up on the table. If the lamp has a shade, take it off. Turn on the light. This is your sun.

5 Sit or kneel in the middle of the square. Your head should be just above the edge of the tables.

YOU ARE HERE

6 Set your moon on Table 2. Look straight at it from the middle of the square. How much of the marshmallow has light shining on it that you can see from where you are? Eat the marshmallow on the table to match the lighted area of the moon on the stick. (**Hint:** Half of what you see should be lit and half should be dark. That means you eat half the marshmallow). This is called a quarter moon. You see a quarter moon when the moon and sun are about a quarter of a circle away from each other. This means they rise and set from four to eight hours apart, depending on the time of the year.

1

7 Move the moon to Table 3, opposite the sun. Look straight at it from the middle of the square. How much of the marshmallow has light shining on it? Eat the marshmallow on the table to match the lighted area of the one on the stick. (**Hint:** All of what you see should be lit. That means you won't eat any!) When the moon rises just as the sun is setting, you see one whole side of the moon. This is called a full moon. Put the full moon marshmallow back on the table.

4   2

3

8 Move the moon on a stick to Table 4. Look straight at it from the middle of the square. How much of the marshmallow has light shining on it? Eat the marshmallow on the table to match. Put your moon phase marshmallow on the table. This is another quarter moon.

9 Move the moon on a stick to Table 1 right in front of the sun. Look straight at it from the middle of the square. How much of the marshmallow do you see with light shining on it? Eat the marshmallow so that it matches the lighted part of the moon on the stick. (**Hint:** All of what you see should be dark. That means you eat it all!) When the moon rises at the same time as the sun, you don't see the moon. This is called a new moon.

NOTE: If you put your moon on a stick between the new moon and quarter moon marshmallows, you would see the crescent moon phase. If you put your moon on a stick between the quarter moon and full moon marshmallows, you would see the gibbous phase.

ACTIVITY: **Build a Personal Stardome**

SUPPLIES

- ✧ dark umbrella
- ✧ measuring tape
- ✧ chalk
- ✧ star pattern template (nomadpress.net/ resources)
- ✧ glow-in-the-dark paint
- ✧ damp cloth

For thousands of years, people have used constellations as a compass, calendar, and clock. By making and using a personal stardome, you can learn to identify eight constellations. You can also learn to tell direction using one easy-to-find constellation.

1 Open the umbrella. Put one end of the measuring tape near the center post inside the umbrella. Stretch it along a metal rib to an outside edge. Write down the distance.

2 Divide this distance by eight.

3 Using this number, the tape measure, and chalk, mark eight dots at the same distance along each rib. Connect the dots to make eight even circles.

4 Use the glow-in-the-dark paint to label each pie-shaped wedge between two ribs. Labels should be A, B, C, D, E, F, G, and H.

5 Use chalk to copy the star patterns. If you make a mistake, erase it with a damp cloth.

6 When you like how the star patterns look, paint over the chalk stars. Let the paint dry before closing your personal star dome.

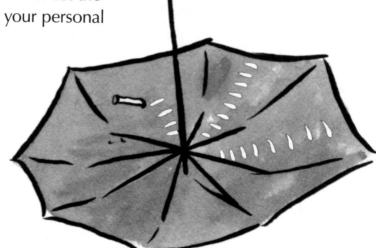

CONSTELLATION PATTERNS	
Wedge A	Orion: the Hunter
Wedge B	Polaris: the North Star Cassiopeia: the Queen Pegasus: the Winged Horse
Wedge C	Pegasus: the Winged Horse
Wedge D	Lyra: a Stringed Instrument
Wedge E	Corona Borealis: the Northern Crown
Wedge F	Ursa Major: the Big Dipper
Wedge G	Ursa Major: the Big Dipper
Wedge H	Gemini: the Twins Canis Major: the Big Dog

USING YOUR STAR DOME: Open your star dome near a chair. Put wedge B so you can see it over the top of the chair. Crouch down and tilt the handle until you see the Big Dipper barely above the top of the chair. This is what the night sky would look like around September 1 at 8 p.m. in the Northern Hemisphere. Slowly turn the handle counterclockwise to the left. The stars near the center will always be visible when you look at the night sky to the north. The stars near the edge will appear to rise and set. These are the ones that look like they go straight above your head outside. In a 12-hour night (8 p.m. to 8 a.m.), you would be able to see almost five sections of stars.

ACTIVITY: **Make a Human Compass**

The two stars that create the front side of the Big Dipper's cup are known as the pointer stars because they point to Polaris, the North Star. Now you can turn yourself into a compass simply by looking up at the sky at night!

1 Look up at the Big Dipper and imagine drawing a line from the star at the bottom of the cup, through the star on the top of the cup and keep on going. The next brightest star you will find on this line is Polaris, the North Star. This is the single star painted closest to the middle pole on your stardome.

2 If you are outside looking straight at Polaris, you are looking north. Your back is facing south. Lift your right arm straight out to the side. It is pointing east. Lift your left arm straight out to the side. It is pointing west. You are now a human compass.

EYE TEST

In ancient Rome, you had to pass an eye test to be an archer in the army. A general would take you outside on a clear night. You would be asked how many stars you saw in the handle of the Big Dipper. How many stars do you see? Some people see three stars. Others see four. In the middle of the handle, there are two stars that look close to each other. If you can see both of these without glasses, you could have been a Roman archer.

ACTIVITY: **Bouncing Beams of Light**

Why are most reflectors made of many small pieces instead of just one giant piece? So the reflected light doesn't blind you!

1 Wrap a piece of foil over the front of the book. Try to keep it smooth. Stand the book up.

2 Put your head level with the book. Hold the flashlight next to one eye. Point the flashlight toward the foil and turn it on. Ouch! The light bounces back straight into your eyes.

3 Now hold the flashlight off to one side and point it towards the foil. Keep your head in the middle. The light is reflected, but off to the other side. That doesn't help you see things better.

4 Take the foil off the book. Crumple it up, then smooth it out. Wrap it over the front of the book again.

5 Stand the book up. Put your head level with the book. Hold the flashlight next to one eye. Point it towards the foil and turn on the flashlight. That's better. You can see the light, but it doesn't hurt.

6 Go outside with your flashlight. What can you find that reflects? Notice how it is made to keep it from hurting your eyes.

NOTE: Since we don't want to get blinded by reflected light, reflectors are made so the light gets bounced in many ways. Using many small reflectors also lets designers point the reflectors in many directions. That way, they can reflect light coming from many different directions.

ACTIVITY: **Firefly Fun**

There are over 2,000 kinds of fireflies in the world. Each type of firefly has its own pattern of flashes. Fireflies find a mate by looking for a matching flash pattern. There are some fireflies that do the wrong pattern on purpose. Then they eat the fireflies that come near.

1 Put the index cards into two piles of five cards each. Label the cards in one pile "boy." Label the cards in the other pile "girl."

2 Draw matching codes on each set of cards.

- 1: dot, dot, dot
- 2: dot, dot, dash
- 3: dot, dash, dash
- 4: dash, dot, dash
- 5: dash, dash, dash

3 Use the glue to make big bumps on the dots. Make big lines for the dashes. Let the glue dry.

 1

 2

 3

 4

 5

DID YOU KNOW?

There are some female Photuris fireflies that will kill and eat other kinds of male fireflies. Fireflies are the only known night-flying insects that hunt.

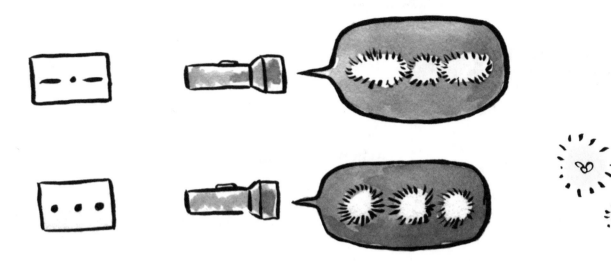

4 Put the cards face down. Every kid picks a card and looks at it, but does not show it to anyone else. If the card says boy, you will be moving around during the game. If the card says girl, you will find a place in the open to sit and wait during the game.

5 Everyone has 20 seconds to go into the dark with their flashlight and card. After 20 seconds, all the players start flashing their codes. Look at the other flashes. Wait five seconds before flashing again.

6 The people with boy cards can move to where they see a flashing match. But watch out! If the codes don't match, the girl firefly will eat the non-matching boy for dinner and that player is out.

7 The game is over when everyone has found their match or has been eaten. Mix up the cards and play again.

CLASSROOM CONNECTION: Fireflies glow to warn predators of the poisons they contain that taste bad. Play firefly tag at recess. Scatter light sources around, such as flashlights and glowsticks. When the tagger tries to get you, grab a light and you're safe. If you don't have a light, the trapper "eats" you and you're out. Play until one firefly is left.

ACTIVITY: **Night Science Mad Lib**

SUPPLIES

✧ glossary (next page)
✧ pencil

Use as many glossary words as you can to fill in the blanks and complete this silly story about night. Try reading it at bedtime when you're done.

_____ Saves the Night!
_{YOUR NAME}

Big Dipper, _____ of the night sky was _____ . It was almost _____ and
_{NOUN} _{ADJECTIVE} _{TIME OF DAY}

the _____ was nowhere to be seen. Where was it? "I would give my right _____ to
_{NOUN} _{NOUN}

know what is going on!" shouted Big Dipper. "Doesn't anyone know how to _____ ?"
_{VERB}

All the _____ hid under their _____ . They had never seen Big Dipper so _____ .
_{PLURAL NOUN} _{PLURAL NOUN} _{ADJECTIVE}

"Maybe _____ would help," said a _____ .
_{"ING" VERB} _{NOUN}

"That's a _____ , " said a _____ .
_{ADJECTIVE} _{NOUN}

Suddenly, _____ came crashing out of the _____ _____ . Everyone
_{YOUR NAME} _{ADJECTIVE} _{NOUN}

started _____ _____ . "I see you have a _____ . It's okay. All you have
_{"ING" VERB} _{ADVERB} _{NOUN}

to do is _____ a _____ ," said _____ .
_{VERB} _{NOUN} _{YOUR NAME}

The _____ looked at each other. Then they started to _____ .
_{PLURAL NOUN} _{VERB}

After _____ _____ , they were done. They took their _____ to Big
_{NUMBER} _{TIME PERIOD} _{NOUN}

Dipper who was very _____ . "Who thought of this?" _____ Big Dipper.
_{ADJECTIVE} _{VERB}

"_____ did!" said the _____ .
_{YOUR NAME} _{PLURAL NOUN}

"As a reward, I will make a _____ out of _____ in the night sky. _____
_{NOUN} _{NOUN} _{PLURAL NOUN}

everywhere will see it and remember what _____ did," said Big Dipper.
_{YOUR NAME}

That is why if you _____ _____ at the night sky, you might _____
_{VERB} _{ADVERB} _{VERB}

a _____ _____ .
_{ADJECTIVE} _{NOUN}

86

Glossary

abdomen: one of three parts of a beetle that is located after its hind legs.

absorb: to soak up a liquid or take in energy, heat, light, or sound.

adaptation: something that helps a plant or animal survive.

amphibian: an animal with moist skin that is born in water but lives on land. An amphibian changes its body temperature by moving to warmer or cooler places. Frogs, toads, newts, efts, and salamanders are amphibians.

antenna: one of two moveable feelers on an insect's head that it uses mainly for smelling. It can also be used for sensing touch, heat, sound, and taste. Plural is antennae.

asteroid: a small rocky object orbiting the sun. Asteroids are too small to be planets.

astronomer: a person who studies the stars, planets, and other things in space.

atmosphere: the layer of gases that wraps around the earth.

bioluminescent: when living things give off light.

cartilage: the stiff, flexible parts of the nose and ear.

cell: the most basic part of a living thing. Billions of cells make up a plant or animal.

chemical: a substance that has certain features that can react with other substances.

communicate: to share information in some way, such as sounds, words, or actions.

condensation: when water vapor sticks together to make droplets.

cone cell: a cone-shaped cell in the retina that is sensitive to bright light and color.

constellation: a group of stars that form a shape or pattern. There are 88 official constellations in the sky.

cue: a signal.

dawn: the time before the sun rises above the horizon, when there is sunlight in the sky.

depth perception: being able to tell how close or far away something is.

dew: water droplets made when humid air cools at night.

dusk: the time after the sun goes below the horizon, when there is still sunlight in the sky.

eardrum: a tight flap of skin that separates the middle ear from the outer ear.

echolocation: finding things by sending out sound waves and listening for them to bounce back.

equator: an imaginary line around the middle of the earth that divides it in two halves.

equinox: a Latin word than means "equal night." The spring equinox is around March 21 and the fall equinox is around September 23. On these two days each year, day and night are 12 hours long all around the world.

Glossary

external: on the outside.

frequency: the number of sound waves that pass a specific point each second.

frost: water from the air that forms tiny ice crystals on cold surfaces at night.

fungus: a plant-like living thing without leaves or flowers. It grows on plants and things that are rotting, like old logs. Examples are mold, mildew, and mushrooms. Plural is fungi.

galaxy: a group of millions or billions of stars. The earth is in a galaxy called the Milky Way.

gland: a sac that makes and releases substances the body needs.

horizon: the line that separates the land from the sky.

humidity: the amount of water in the air.

iris: a part of the eye with a muscle that is seen as a ring of color.

larva: the worm form of an insect. Plural is larvae.

light pollution: too much man-made light during the night from street lights, signs, and buildings, so that it is hard to see stars. Plants and animals can act differently when there is too much light at night.

light source: the place where light is coming from.

light year: a unit of measure for very long distances. One light year is the distance that light travels in a year, about 6 trillion miles (9.5 trillion kilometers).

mammal: an animal that has a constant body temperature and is mostly covered with hair or fur. Humans, dogs, horses, and mice are mammals.

meteorite: any piece of space material that makes it to the surface of the earth after falling through the atmosphere.

meteor: the streak of light when a small rock or piece of dust burns up as it enters the earth's atmosphere. We see it as a shooting star.

migrate: to move from one place to another.

nerve: a group of cells bundled together like a wire that sends messages to the brain.

neuron: a special cell that sends electrical and chemical messages to your brain.

night science: the study of the natural world at night.

night: the time after the sun sets and before the sun rises, when it is dark.

nocturnal: active at night.

Northern Hemisphere: the half of the earth north of the equator.

North Pole: the most northern point on the earth.

orbit: the path the earth takes as it circles the sun.

organ: a part of the body with a special function, like the heart, lungs, brain, and skin.

peripheral: at the side or edge of something.

pinna: the skin and cartilage that collects sound waves around the ear. Humans have two pinnae.

predator: an animal that hunts other animals for food.

prey: an animal that is hunted by another animal.

pupil: the opening that lets light into the eye.

reflector: a piece of glass, metal, or other material that sends, or reflects, light back.

reflect: to redirect something that hits a surface, such as heat, light, or sound.

reptile: an animal covered with scales that crawls on its belly or on short legs. A reptile changes its body temperature by moving to warmer or cooler places. Snakes, turtles, lizards, alligators, and crocodiles are reptiles.

retina: the light-sensitive lining at the back of the eye.

rod cell: a rod-shaped cell in the retina that is sensitive to low light. It cannot pick up colors.

senses: seeing, hearing, smelling, touching, and tasting. These are ways that people and animals get information about the world around them.

sensitive: easily affected by something.

shadow: an area that looks dark because something is between it and the light.

silhouette: a real object that looks dark because the light is behind it.

solstice: a Latin word that means "sun stands still." This happens when the earth tilts as far as it can toward or away from the sun. It is when the sun is highest in the sky in the summer, and lowest in the sky in the winter.

sound waves: invisible vibrations that you hear as sound.

Southern Hemisphere: the half of the earth south of the equator.

South Pole: the most southern point on the earth.

spore: a tiny one-celled living thing produced by fungi. It is like an egg, because it can grow into an adult of the fungus.

supernova: an exploding star.

tapetum lucidum: a special layer of cells found behind the retina in many animals' eyes. These cells reflect light.

twilight: light that is visible in the sky at dawn and dusk, when the sun is below the horizon.

vibrate: to move back and forth very, very quickly.

water vapor: water as a gas, like fog, steam, or mist.

wavelength: the spacing of sound waves. It is measured by the distance from the high point of one wave to the high point of the next wave.

whisker: a thick, stiff hair that has extra touch receptors at its base.

Resources

Books

Almoznino, Albert. *The Art of Hand Shadows*. Dover Publications, 2002.

Branley, Franklyn M. *What Makes Day and Night (Let's Read and Find Out Science 2)*. Collins, 1986.

Branley, Franklyn M. *The Moon Seems to Change (Let's Read and Find Out Science 2)*. Collins, 1987.

Colburn, Cherie Foster. *Our Shadow Garden*. Bright Sky Press, 2010.

Elliot, Lang. *A Guide to Night Sounds: The Nighttime Sounds of 60 Mammals, Birds, Amphibians, and Insects*. Stackpole Books, 2004.

Landry, Sarah. *Peterson First Guide to Urban Wildlife*. Houghton Mifflin Harcourt, 1998.

Love, Ann and Jane Drake. *The Kids Book of the Night Sky*. Kids Can Press, 2004.

Mattern, Joanne. *The Pebble First Guide to Nocturnal Animals*. Capstone Press, 2009.

O'Neill, Mary Le Duc. *The Sound of Day, the Sound of Night*. Farrar, Strauss and Giroux, 2003.

Opler, Paul A. *Peterson First Guide to Butterflies and Moths*. Houghton Mifflin Harcourt, 1998.

Sasaki, Chris. *Constellations: A Glow-in-the-Dark Guide to the Night Sky*. Sterling Publishing, 2006.

Schoberle, Cecile. *Day lights, night lights*. Simon & Schuster Books for Young Readers, 1994.

Yolen, Jane. *Owl Moon*. Philomel, 1987.

Web Sites

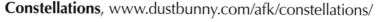

Almanac for Kids, www.almanac4kids.com/

Constellations, www.dustbunny.com/afk/constellations/

Day and Night map, www.fourmilab.ch/cgi-bin/uncgi/Earth/action?opt=-p&img=learth.evif

Frog and toad calls, www.naturesound.com/frogs/frogs.html

Globe at Night, www.globeatnight.org

Owl calls, www.owlpages.com/sounds.php

The Sky Tonight, www.kidsastronomy.com/astroskymap/index.htm

Songs of Insects, www.musicofnature.org/songsofinsects/

What a Wonderful World Shadow Show, www.youtube.com/watch?v=EAQxNVQF_I0

Index